BEARINGS

PRINCETON A.   [ARCHITECTURAL PRESS]
PARSONS SCHOOL OF DESIGN

Published by
Princeton Architectural Press
37 East 7th Street
New York, New York 10003
212.995.9620

ISBN 1-878271-28-8
© Princeton Architectural Press
All rights reserved.
94 93 92 91 4 3 2 1
Printed and bound in the United States.

Book design: Kevin Lippert
Production editor: Stefanie Lew
Special thanks to: Scott Corbin, Sheila Cohen,
Antje Fritsch, Clare Jacobson, and Ann Urban

Library of Congress Cataloguing-in Publicaion Data

Bearings
Organizers
Deborah Gans, Parsons School of Design; Pratt Institute
Patricia C. Phillips, Parsons School of Design
Mark Robbins, Ohio State University
Exhibition Curator
Keller Easterling, Parsons School of Design; Pratt Institute
Publication Editor
Stefanie Lew

Department of Environmental Design
James Wines, Chairperson
Marta Gutman, Associate Chairperson
Patricia C. Phillips, Assistant Chairperson
Grant Taylor, Department Administrator

Parsons School of Design
Charles Olton, Dean
Lesley Cadman, Associate Dean
David C. Levy, Chancellor of the University and
Chancellor for the Arts

Acknowledgments

The *Bearings* exhibitions and this catalogue have been
possible through the generous support of the Graham
Foundation for Advanced Studies in the Fine Arts and the
New York State Council on the Arts.
Thanks to Clinton Kuopus, Director of the Parsons Exhibi-
tion Center, and his student staff for their assistance with
the exhibitions. Thanks also to Linda Levy Anzer, Angel
Gonzalez, and the Parsons Publication Design staff for a
memorable poster design.
Thanks to Scott Joyce, a student in the Environmental
Design Department, who helped with this project.
Credit to Grant Taylor for photography for Deborah Gans,
Brian McGrath, Mark Robbins, and Benjamin Gianni.
Photograph on page 35 © Craig Kumner.
Special thanks to the Estate of Andre Kertesz for use of
the photograph, "Disappearing Act" (1955).

Bearings 1988-89
Parsons Exhibition Center
7 December 1988–7 January 1989

Jurors
Marta Gutman, Associate Chairperson, Department of Environmental Design, Parsons School of Design
Alberto Perez-Gomez, Saidye Rosner Bronfman Professor of the History of Architecture, McGill University
Michael Sorkin, Visiting Professor, Columbia University, Cooper Union; Architecture Critic, *The Village Voice*
Susana Torre, Associate Professor, School of Architecture, Preservation, and Planning, Columbia University
John Whiteman, Director, The S.O.M. Foundation, Chicago Institute for Architecture and Urbanism

Exhibitors
Marc M. Angelil, University of Southern California
Karen Bausman and **Leslie Gill,** Parsons School of Design
Susan Bower and **Stephen Leet,** Parsons School of Design and New York Institute of Technology
Michael Carey Cranfill, University of Kentucky
Deborah Gans, Pratt Institute
Gisue Hariri and **Mojgan Hariri,** Columbia University
John P. Maruszczak, University of Texas at Arlington
Brian McGrath, New Jersey Institute of Technology
Taeg Nishimoto, Pratt Institute; New York Institute of Technology
Mark O'Bryan, Ohio State University
Mark Robbins, Parsons School of Design
Joel Sanders and **Scott Sherk,** Princeton University and Muhlenberg College
Terence Van Elslander, Rensselaer Polytechnic Institute
Mark West, Carleton University

Note: Institutional affiliation for jurors and exhibitors are listed for the 1988–89 academic year.

Bearings 1990-91
Parsons Exhibition Center
16 January–8 February 1991

Jurors
Mildred Freidman, Curator of Design, Walker Art Center
Miriam Gusevich, Architect and Planner, Chicago Park District; Professor, University of Illinois
Patricia C. Phillips, Assistant Chairperson, Department of Environmental Design, Parsons School of Design; Critic, *Artforum*
Martin Puryear, Sculptor
Ricardo Scofidio, Professor, School of Architecture, Cooper Union; Architect, Diller + Scofidio

Exhibitors
Robert Cole, Catholic University
Benjamin Gianni, Ohio State University
Cameron McNall, Otis Art Institute of Parsons School of Design
Wellington Reiter, Harvard University; MIT

CONTENTS

INTRODUCTION

Marta Gutman

The Department of Environmental Design at Parsons School of Design welcomes *Bearings*, the catalogue of architectural work displayed in the first two exhibitions of the same name. In 1988 Patricia C. Phillips, then Associate Chair of the department; Mark Robbins; and Keller Easterling first conceived of a juried exhibition of North American architectural design work partially or fully developed through the designer's involvement with teaching. The group, drawing in part on their pedagogic experiences in this department, surmised that student-teacher exchange leads to speculative, inventive design, rich in intellectual and philosophical issues. The resulting exhibition of strong and provocative faculty work confirmed their premise, leading them to organize a second exhibition and a publication of the exhibitors' work from both *Bearings*.

On behalf of the department, I would like to thank the group for pursuing the *Bearings* project. The catalogue stands as a thoughtful record of the design work shown in the two exhibitions. Here, as there, the excellent design work draws the readers/viewers into creative dialogue and exchange as it challenges them to surpass its high standards.

The department would also like to thank the many other people and organizations who helped make this publication and the *Bearings* exhibitions possible, including all the individuals who submitted work for consideration; the distinguished jury members (listed elsewhere in this publication); Clinton Kuopus, Director of the Parsons Exhibition Center and his student staff; and Kevin Lippert, Stefanie Lew, and the staff of Princeton Architectural Press. Funding was generously provided by the Graham Foundation for Advanced Studies in the Fine Arts and the New York State Council on the Arts.

BEARINGS

Patricia C. Phillips

Bearings is constructed as a biennial call for entries. Teachers from undergraduate and graduate programs of architecture and design in North America are invited to submit portfolios. The work, accomplished in the past three years, may include theoretical, speculative, or built projects, but it must make some attempt to demonstrate a personal vision as it relates to a philosophy of teaching—a pedagogical process.

Bearings attempts to present a range of work and issues under consideration by design instructors. The biennial is an opportunity to examine not only the connections of teaching and individual work, but to gauge the influences of region, architectural theory, and other sources on contemporary ideas, production, and pedagogy.

Over the years, the submission guidelines for *Bearings* have remained unchanged with two exceptions. The first call for entries was directed at young teachers who had taught no more than seven years. The second *Bearings* invited all instructors from accredited programs of architecture or design to participate. The initial restriction now seems an error—an unnecessary limitation of variables and possible "findings."

The second adjustment involves teaching documents. While the first call for entries asked solely for a portfolio of individual creative work, the 1990-91 *Bearings* asked for a presentation of recent projects, but also required specific evidence of pedagogical position. Entrants were asked to include two (proposed or realized) academic or studio programs. This amendment attempts to demonstrate more clearly the (still slippery) connections of teaching and individual work, and intensifies the project's focus on the quality and nature of this dialogue.

We hope that successive *Bearings* continue to improve the methods of discovery so that the findings may suggest more insistent questions about creative activity and critical education, about making and teaching.

GETTING ONE'S

Patricia C. Phillips

"The great men and women of culture are those who have had a passion for diffusing, for making prevail, for carrying from one end of society to the other, the best knowledge, the best ideas of their time . . . "
—Matthew Arnold, *Culture and Anarchy*

As a critic I sometimes stand in the ambiguously attached position of the peripheral, curious observer of some process or event. The "critical distance" suggests an enlarged scope of vision, a gaze that may catch more light and focus. Distance provides and broadens—and it protects and deforms. Political scientist Michael Walzer writes in *The Company of Critics* about the "connected critic" who accomplishes an incisive perspective through passionate interest and involvement in a community. He looks at an activity of social criticism and observation which does not require or condone indifference and separation. For this particular essay the idea of "connection" is not just a goal—it is a condition; I can pretend no detachment here.

Several years ago, Mark Robbins, who was at that time a faculty member at Parsons School of Design, suggested a national action—a call for entries—that might shed some light on the evasive questions of architecture and pedagogy. Others joined the dialogue and a clearer mission, strategy, and name (thanks to exhibition curator Keller Easterling) emerged.

Bearings is a process of looking and locating. It began in a department of architecture and design that has struggled to situate itself in the generous geography of art and design education. Neither a professional program in architecture nor a traditional interior design program, Environmental Design at Parsons has sought a difficult, dynamic synthesis of art, architecture, and design with contemporary social events and cultural phenomena. Parsons has sought a supple curriculum that encourages cross-disciplinary investigation and individual imagination. Its definition has been a long labor of orientation.

It is in this skeptical, academic climate that *Bearings* became a biennial research project. It remains, in some ways, a vehicle to see the current preoccupations of schools of architecture and design in North America, to study issues that share common ground as well as how institutional structure and region shape more localized concerns. The method of observation—and *Bearings'* central mission—is the review of work of faculty members in various schools and programs. It has been the biennial's objective to seek connections—not just to look at one thing but to consider how a range of cultural and environmental factors affect teaching and practice. The process appeals for a cross-section of faculty portfolios of current work (built projects as well as speculation and theory) so that the competition jurors, the design professions, and the public may envision how the creative process relates to pedagogical method.

I remain excited by the potential of *Bearings* but accept the great difficulty of its intentions. How, in fact, are these fragile, sometimes ambivalent connections between artistic work, teaching, region, program, and institutional situation presented and visualized? *Bearings*, a speculative project, gathers data from a broad sampling of architects/artists/teachers. The processes of submission and review encourage self-reflection, but they leave the paths of investigation and hypothesis to each observer.

The research is directed by the belief that all teachers must strive for the demanding life of creative activity, as well as a passionate commitment to an aesthetic, critical education. In my role at Parsons, I have spent many hours in the past seven years sitting with architects, artists, and designers who want to teach. There are recurrent themes and itineraries for these interviews: the discussion of program, the prospective teacher's philosophy, an attitude about the studio process, and a review of the portfolio of work (and occasionally students' work produced in another teaching position).

The difficult task is to discern connections, to speculate about an untested teacher or the agility of an experienced critic in a new context. Sometimes there is a stunning portfolio, but a disturbing indifference to teaching, a scant consideration of the demands of pedagogical dialogue. Other times, there is a clear enthusiasm for the challenges of the seminar or studio, an appreciation for the improvisations that each new student, course, and year require, but sparse evidence of energetic, searching work.

There are ample examples of teachers who have let one dimension of this tense dialectic retreat while the other may progress spectacularly. *Bearings* is a look at general creative and pedagogical locations, as well as current pressure systems—restless, disturbed atmospheres that force new issues of inquiry, teaching, and creative work. At times, I have felt that *Bearings* asks vague, insoluble questions, but it meditates—and sometimes eloquently—on the passage to being an architect/artist who teaches, the pursuit of the most challenging ideas in one's work, and the generous projection of this impassioned curiosity to a group of students. *Bearings* is a project to honor the mapped and unmarked routes of critical pedagogy.

MARC M. ANGELIL

Process and Experimentation

The studio or atelier is the place in which ideas are conceived and brought into form. Hypotheses are tested, rejected, and newly formulated. In this sense, the architectural product that is created can be seen in close affinity to the process of design. The studio as the locus for making architecture offers a framework for understanding the fundamental relationship between the means and ends of architectural undertakings. A primary objective of design, in other words, pertains to the investigation of the processes which contribute to the formulation of architecture.

Design as a method of production consequently engages in a search towards the definition of new solutions. Analogous to the concept of the scientific laboratory experiment, the architectural design process, in the context of the studio environment, encompasses this idea of experimentation. Design work considered from the vantage point of experimental undertaking suggests the possibilities for searching and revealing. Ultimately, experimentation can be considered as a mode of operation in the process of design. Experimentation challenges, by definition, the established order of things. Preconceived notions about architecture and established conventions are put into question. Such an approach to design necessitates a conscious effort and the willingness to take risks. "The need to run certain risks," Theodor Adorno asserts, "is actualized in the idea of experimentation." Experimentation allows new territory to be explored in what is often a difficult search. While including the concept of experimentation, investigations of process imply an awareness of the specific techniques involved in production. Technical design skills must be considered in view of ideas, concepts, and intellectual constructs in order to achieve a meaningful architecture. Only with such a framework in which theoretical and practical considerations are merged can an investigation within the nature of process be identified. Process is herein founded on the understanding of design as a constructive method, including both intellectual and physical frameworks. Adorno writes: "Construction necessitates solutions that are not immediately present or obvious to the senses." Within construction, he continues, "the unforeseen, then, not only is a contingent effect, but also has a moment of objectivity." In that idea a connection is established between experimentation as an operational strategy and design as a constructive method.

The work presented involves an exploration of the interdependence of design process and design product. Procedures, techniques, and methods of making architecture are investigated in relation to the architectural object. An awareness of the instruments involved in the process of design is emphasized; the pencil and ink drawing and the model are used as precise tools and contrasted with the framework of design processes, attempting a synthesis between material project and intellectual constructs in the making of architecture. The drawing and the model do not represent a pictorial image of reality, but are instead integral to the procedures of the project.

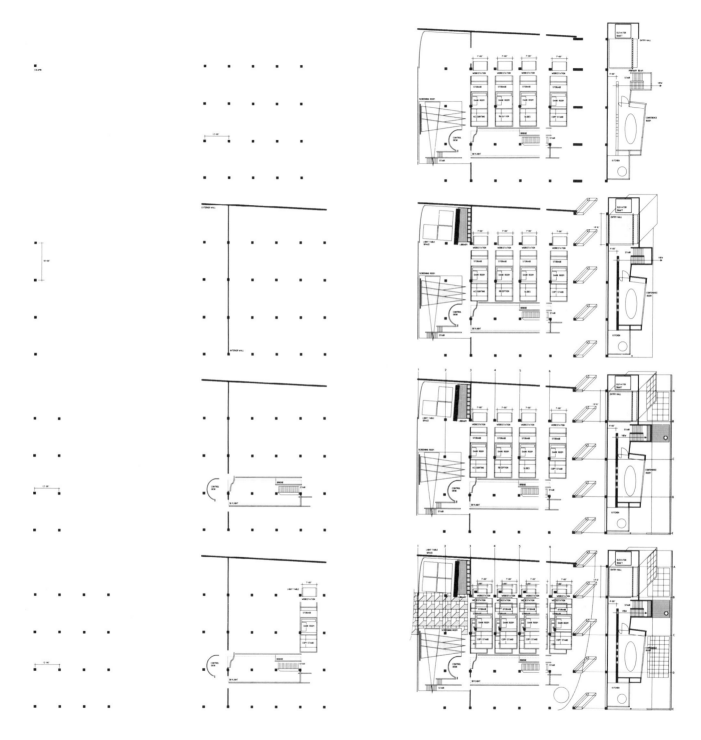

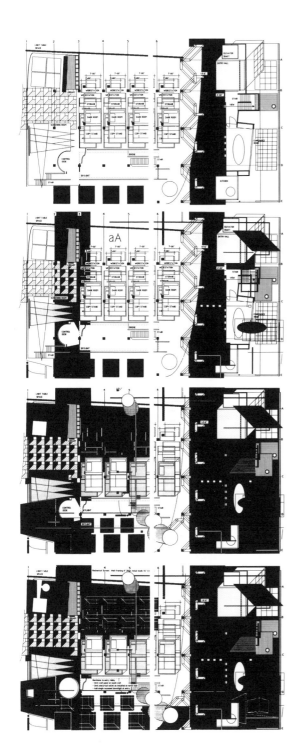
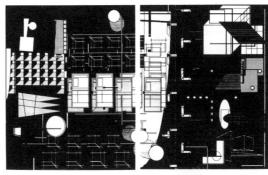
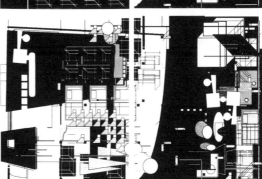
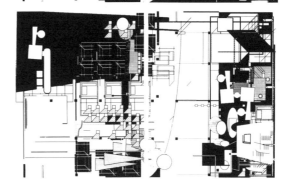
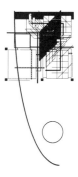

**Investigations
in the Making
of Architecture,**
model and draw-
ing series, with
Sarah R. Graham
and Susan E.
Stevens

BAUSMAN GILL

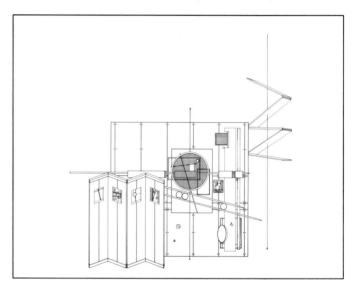

Through the ongoing dialogue of collaboration we actively translate idealized architectural space explored in collage and assemblage form into a body of comprehensible architectural statements, or built work of varying scales.

The small-scaled constructions define the parameters of an imaginary universe. Within this closed system the laws of physics are re-defined. Space, time, gravity, and distance are altered states in each work. This flexible medium allows us to explore and reveal personal statements about a non-scaled architectural landscape.

A series of screens furthers this continued interest in collaged space. At this scale the personalized vision of the construction or box is extended to engage the physical reality of an architectural enclosure. The screen becomes the facade within an interior room, framing views that acknowledge vistas and fragment sight lines.

The constructed windows within form a closed system, an ideal vision employing its own specific gravity, its own telescoping of space. Juxtaposed with the wall of the screen, this sculptural space expands, accentuating the tautness and mass of the surrounding frame. The aim is to continue this expansion, allowing the collaged system to override the surrounding environment.

As a full scale work, the Huxford House best exemplifies this conceptual architectural landscape. The vision of telescoping scale from the massing to the smallest of details and particular use of materials triumphs over the more pragmatic realities of the building.

Opposite page **Lens Screen**
Above **Bam Box #1**
Following pages **Huxford Residence,**
Larchmont, New York, 1987

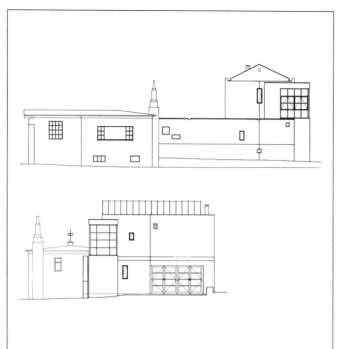

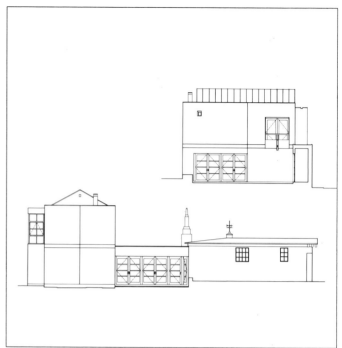

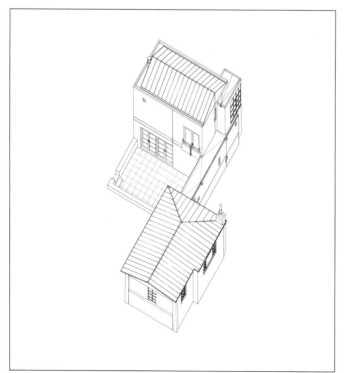

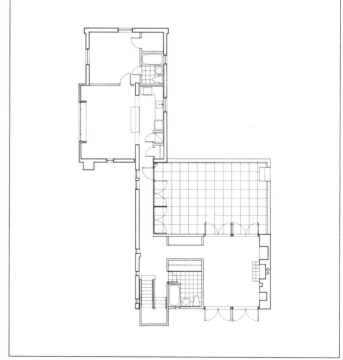

BOWER LEET

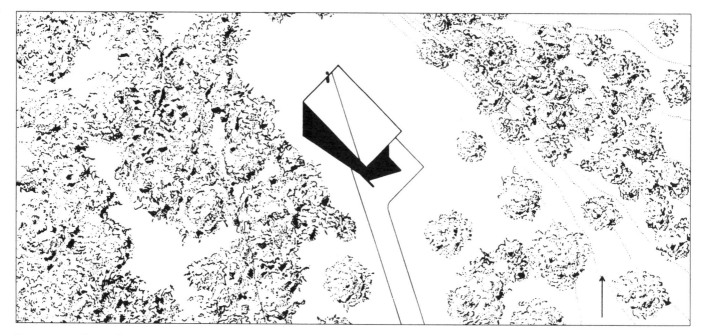

In our work and our teaching we reject the current tendency to confine architecture in restrictive categories—the arcane or mundane, the affirmative or symptomatic, and the poetic or mindless technique. Technique and content, or in other terms, craft and theory must always be reconciled. Neither can be eliminated without destroying architecture's specific virtues. Content is developed and intentional, and must be evident in the work. It is not arbitrary and cannot be added, imported, or over-layed.

We accept both the circumstantial and constant conditions of architecture. The particular and circumstantial restrictions of every architectural "problem" become not limiting determinants of form nor tedious constraints, but are the conditions that initiate exploration and challenge the skills of the architect. At the very least architecture has the capacity to reconcile opposing but not mutually exclusive tendencies: permanence and innovation; program and site; the retinal and tactile; and the structure of space and the structure of form.

In practice and in the design studio, we advocate inquiry through making by developing the ability to recognize the difference between false starts and disclosed discoveries. Acting upon and developing these discoveries hopefully informs our work and the work of our students.

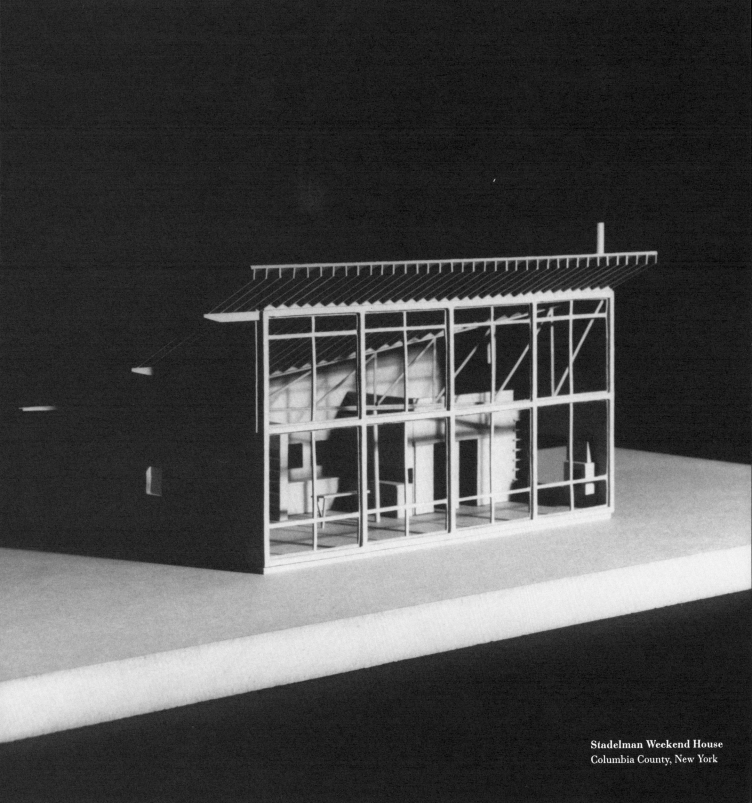

Stadelman Weekend House
Columbia County, New York

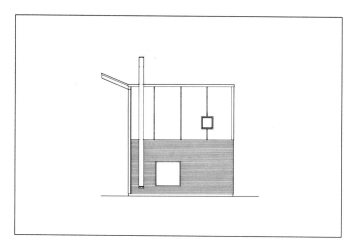

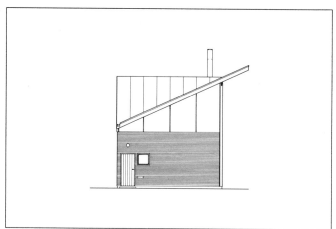

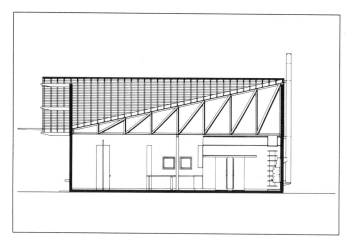

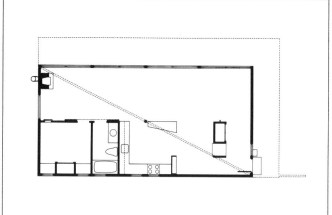

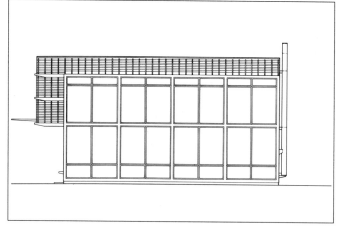

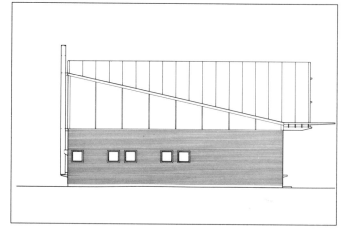

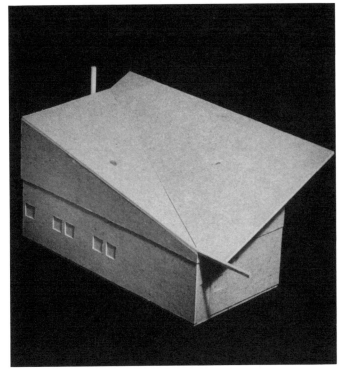

BOWER LEET

From a prison cell the aged Marco Polo diligently recounts his progress in the East, selecting with care the details of the unfamiliar and improbable, not once to shed the imprint of his native Venice, the known quantity against which all is measured. So, too, does Michael Cranfill's destiny carry him to the East, guided by a desire beyond the confines of distance or orientation. Thus guided, Cranfill draws to the surface something which is certainly unfamiliar, albeit grounded in otherwise familiar domains.

"Sand Dragons" is a project conducted over the course of two years in New York, Principal American port of unfamiliar, and his native Kentucky. It is aptly subtitled "Transient Housing"—both the shelters and the anticipated occupants are transient. The site, the marshy land masses of Jamaica Bay, under the shadow of departures from John F. Kennedy International Airport, has informed both the program and the nature of the structures, which mediate land/sea and air, realms of reflection and traversal. Site, program, and structure are each possessed of a corresponding transience; with this remarkable unity of intent we must here consider scale. The passenger jet comes in close overhead, rupturing the vapors, recalling the constellational vision of the outlying King's and Queen's Counties—we are in flight, at night, descending. In this realm are scale-perceptive jets. Architecture embraces the land/sea and is embraced by it. The shelters, new arrivals transfigured cargo—laments to the lost chapels of the airport?—position themselves in this atmosphere in which "other" is native. Their occupation of the marshy dunes mimics the dunes' occupation of the bay, anticipating the disparate sort of (human) occupation that is the formative agent in the history of Venice. As the Venetian "lacuna" serves as the surface of exchange between East and West, so, too, does "Sand Dragons" stand as a witness of exchange between the legendary topographies of China, "vis-a-vis" the geomancer, positioning meanings in the embrace of earth/sea and air, and the imprint of the enveloping, maternal, landscape of Kentucky.

The convergence of these seemingly disparate elements in this project results in an important re-formation of the value of site/model. The site is not modeled as an erasure, an idealized "tabula rasa" whose monological domination of the realm of the "given" is the basis of the essential poverty of current architectural practice, founded as it is upon the tyranny of the plan and bull-dozer; rather, "terra" or landsite, is posited as a corruption upon the stillness of the water. The architect is to re-negotiate a stillness in the corruption implicit to dwelling.

CRANFILL

DEBORAH GANS

Folded Planes

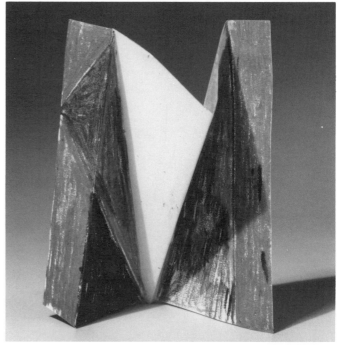

My background is in the fine arts where drawing can be an exploration of marks on paper in relation to the gestures which produce them and to the world of nature which they almost invariably represent. In the representation of architectural design in two dimensions, this magic chemistry of drawing is sometimes forgotten. I try to use drawing in my teaching and in my own work to investigate the conventions of architectural representation and to explore our perception of space. I ask my students to question the idea of frontality in architecture and the relationship of plan or ground plane to elevation or picture plane. We try to understand how plan, section, and elevation are contained in, but transformed by, built architecture.

In the Folded Planes, I physically manipulate the orthogonal relationships of elevation and plan. I think living in New York, where buildings are always to one side of you and very big, impresses upon me the power of the oblique view and the fleeting nature of the right angle, despite the conceptual power of the grid. The folded planes begin as flat depictions of orthogonal spaces such as building and street, trees in forests, mountains and sea. I then re-fold them into three dimensions, but not necessarily according to the spatial divisions of the drawings. In folding, the original image is not lost, but is overlaid with another three-dimensional reality.

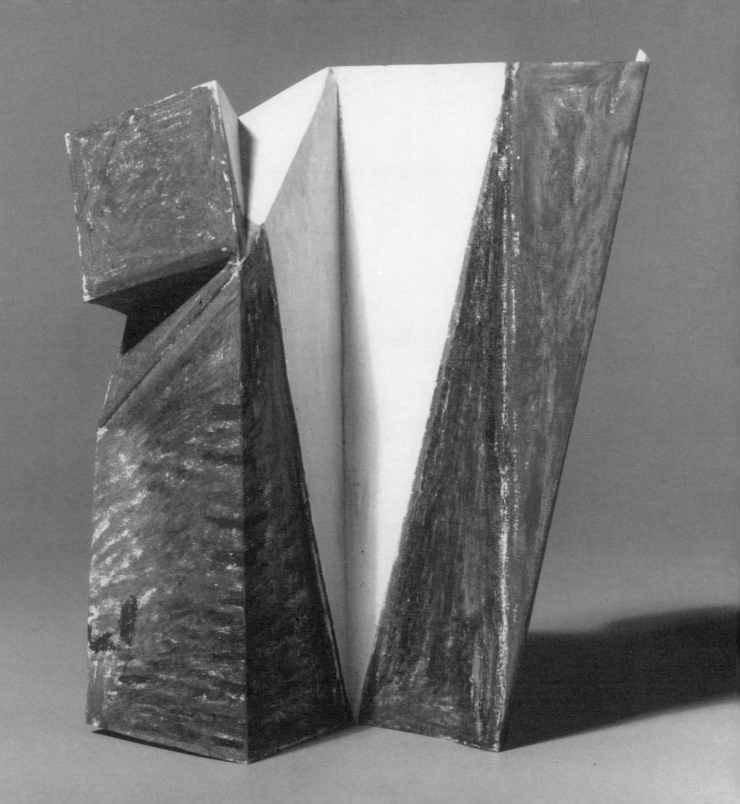

GANS

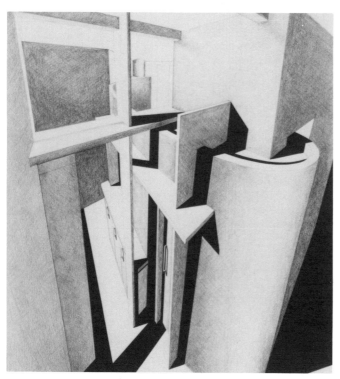

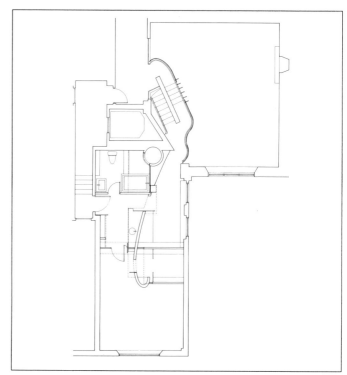

Today the challenge of teaching and practicing architecture is not the communication of a mass of prescribed opinions but rather the direction of a development of poetic sensibility, in the translation of thought into architectural composition, based on a body of findings that have been experienced personally.

This approach rejects the fundamental academic program that, since the Renaissance, has been based on the Aristotelian principle of *deduction*—that all representation is deduced from the general principles of absolute beauty. If deduction is replaced by *induction*, or reasoning from the particular to general, then through the observation of the smallest manifestation of form or energy and the relationship, one can realize the magnitude of natural order. This realization generates a process which enables ideas and imagination to transform into concrete architectural forms. As an alternative mode of expression this generates a base for the development of concepts relating to our evolving perception of space, movement, and time—a base which then allows for harmony and equilibrium free of stylistic imitations.

The selected projects address our philosophical and architectural concerns. Each is a "Hybrid Structure" that fluidly connects a system of interacting spaces and components.

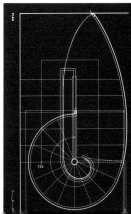

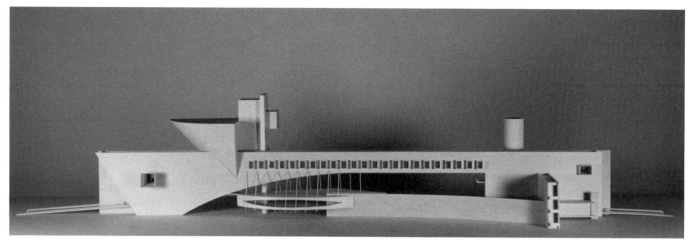

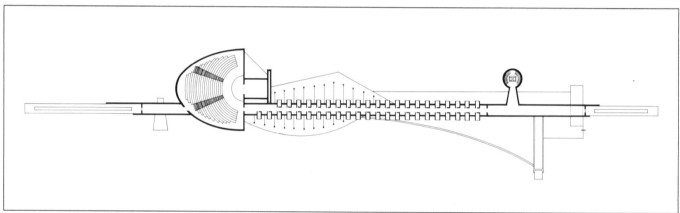

The **DMZ Project** stretches one thousand feet across the demilitarized zone between North and South Korea. Its spine is one hundred feet high and twenty feet wide. The "*structure*" physically takes the form of a "hybrid bridge." It attempts to create a metaphysical path that has no physical destination.

HARIRI & HARIRI

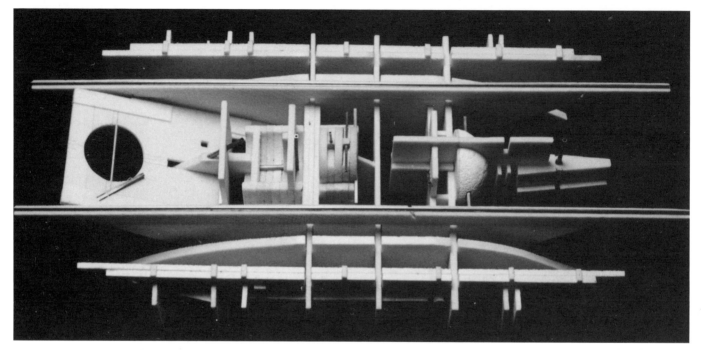

The stories that water can tell within the city and landscape vary from the practical to the symbolic and mythological. The unlimited ability of water to carry metaphor allows for the co-existence of these personae/the existence of this duplicity.

The main theme of this set is the investigation of water as an element of the imagination and its metamorphoses within the city and landscape. Three projects make up the set: Cartographic Waterworks, Topographic Theaters, and The Contracted Landscape. The elements of this water set propose an alternate aqueous infrastructure—Regional (Cartographic Waterworks), the Civic (Topographic Theaters) and the Domestic (The Contracted Landscape).

Therefore the aquatic set is a perceptual key for the storyteller and detective alike, posed as it is between the refraction of a singular droplet and the unlimited resonances of the ocean.

Topographic Theaters
Opposite page
Island Boat
Left
Sky Monitor

Contracted Landscape:
Nelson Addition,
Fort Worth, Texas

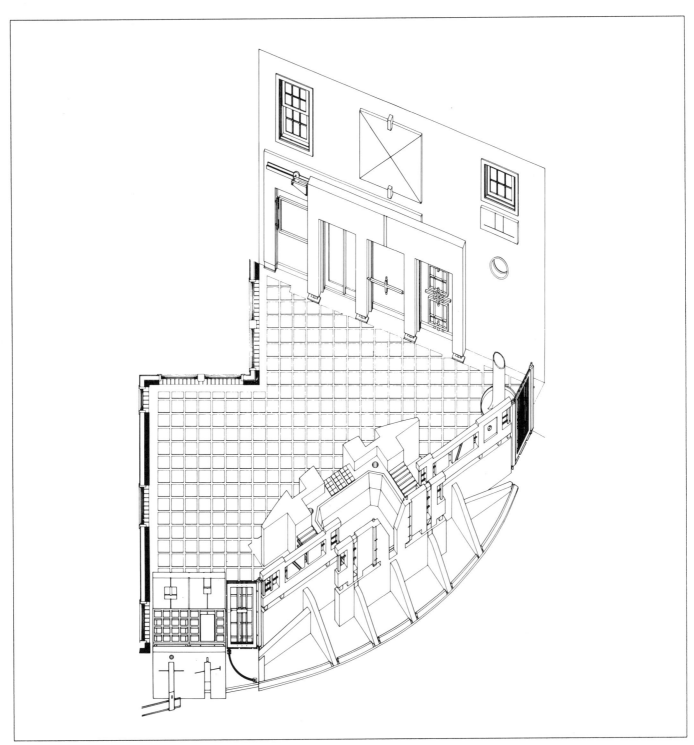

MARUSZCZAK

BRIAN MCGRATH

Safe Sex Piers

(An anti-proposal for non-development: Waterfront
Competition for the Municipal Art Society. 1987)

Four piers on the west side of Manhattan.
Reaching 800 feet into the Hudson River.
Greenwich Village between Morton and Jane Streets.
On the waterfront.
Once the active port for the industrial city.
Ships. Barges. Freight and longshoreman.
America's manufacturing mecca.
Endless basilicas in glass and steel
suspended over the water.
Trusses. Cranes.
Horizontal warehouses as long as the longest ship.

Empty, silent.
Boarded up, abandoned.
Industrial City replaced by World Financial Center.
Manufacturing and shipping now elsewhere.
Neither development nor preservation,
only natural decay and youthful abandonment.
Long empty warehouses,
rotten wood planks reveal the river below.
Darkness in the empty temple to industry.

Silent but for waves,
and the creaks and moans of ghosts.

The waterfront,
becoming: a place for solitude,
to feel alone in the crowded city.
A wooden deck—a nudist's delight.
Inside—fantasy: paintings in empty clerks' offices;
a giant hole carefully cutting an arc through the metal
wall—gash of light in the dark endless hall.
Figures in the shadows, coupled in passion—
a hustler,
a voyeur,
an exhibitionist,
an outcast.
Spontaneous expression at the edge of a desperate city.

Warehouse demolition makes way for a highway that
will never be built.
The developer's march temporarily halted.
The piers now just empty wooden planes shorn of their
cover, rotting at an accelerated pace.
Chain link fences, barbed wire.
A helicopter races gamblers to Atlantic City.
Increasing desperation further off the edge of the city.

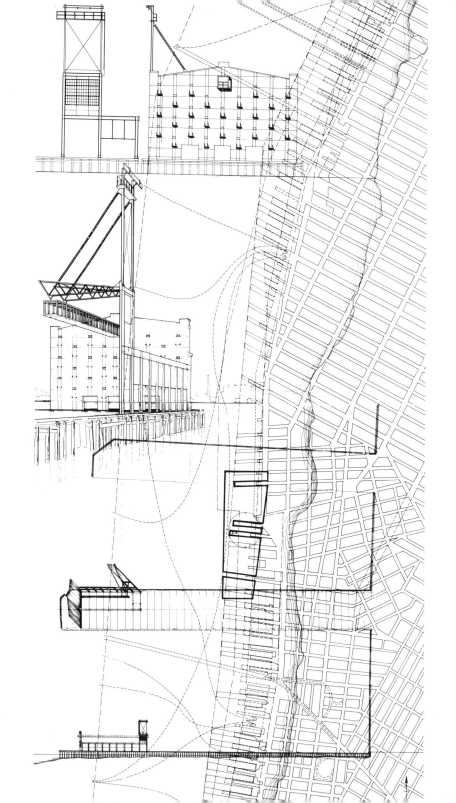

MCGRATH

It is a place (or the sense of place) that one hopes to embody in architecture. Architectural elements are "things" in the sense that they constitute architecture. They bear names both to identify themselves and to place themselves in the context of conceptual reality. They also bear the images that are evoked by the more abstract aspects of their nature.

In an effort to provide architectural imagery, is it possible that an assembly of these elements alone evokes the sense of place? Can a place be specific and imagined, consistent and inconsistent at the same time, like a poet's oneiric descriptions? Is it possible that these "things" create a place by evoking associations?

A composition was attempted by juxtaposing elements in an intentionally non-hierarchical order, which generated a specific geometry and its related tangible and tactile materiality. By keeping the scale of the composition fairly small, each element can be read directly and simultaneously.

Shepherd's Tower

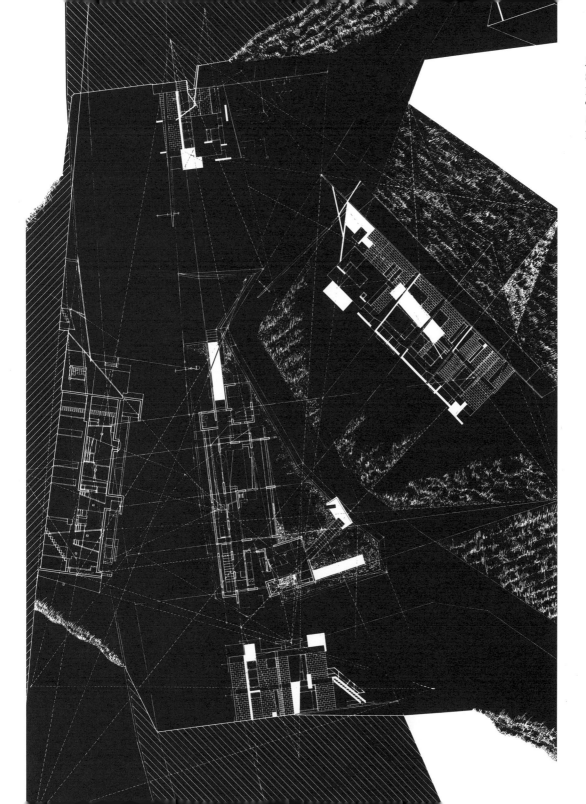

NISHIMOTO

MARK O'BRYAN

"If we consider the geography of this earth, we can begin to understand a few obvious things about it. It is round, as we all can be sure of, finally; it is continuous; it is open and expansive. And though all of this has been known for a long time, it is only recently (the twentieth century) that the experience of this openness is made accessible—it is not exclusive. 'East is east and west is west and never the twain shall meet' is no longer a truth. We have 'seen' primitive cultures and the upheavals (individual and political) of third world countries. What were once unchartered areas are now routinely exposed to us in photographs and media; long-standing traditional ideals are being questioned in the most secure of places. Given the challenge of this visibility, what do we choose to see, and how do we choose to see it?"

Anthony Rocannova
Jerzy Rozenberg

"The architect begins his work, immersed in human history, guided by a sense of its continuity, and focused on the intent and hope of making place an embodiment of the past and future in the present. The landscape as found, by its structure, form, and scale, is given its own particular characteristics of place by time and the seasons, and is the first physical order for the receiving of man-made intervention. Its boundaries are the horizon and the ever-changing plane of the sky. Therefore, a point located in that landscape is fixed and transitory in the beginning. At that moment one is concerned with the simultaneous consideration of order and existence-horizontal and vertical; solid and void; inside, outside, and in between; as well as path and arrival, and the formal disposition of spaces which contain life holding in them memory, speculation, allusion, illusion and wonder. The technical means is assumed and the perception of that possibility in every case predates the technical realization. The drawings and models by which this is studied stand for themselves, but foremost to the maker is that they are the means to architecture."

Paul Pinney

A Pilgrimage Church
on the Island of Corfu

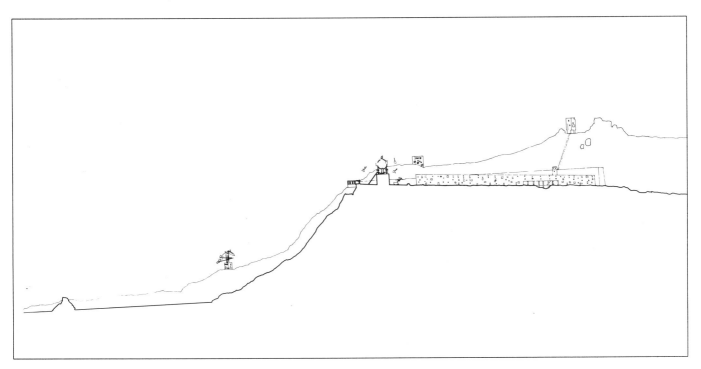

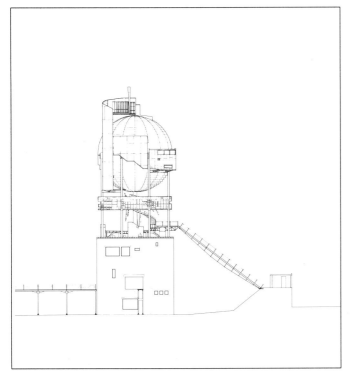

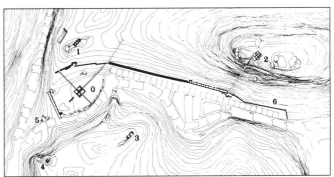

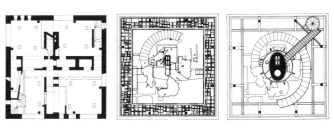

O'BRYAN

MARK ROBBINS

This architectural work is concerned with unveiling the relationships between meaning and form. It employs familiar elements that are repositioned, often as fragments, with forms derived from high and vernacular sources. These references are drawn from a broadly defined formal and cultural vocabulary; they are then manipulated through changes in scale, repetition, and by the use of analogy. The constructions represent many possible readings for the viewer; a constellation of small fires of recognition.

In the studio the architecture student is asked to respond to the world of signs manifest in objects and cities, and to invent within this complex network of associations. The work emphasizes transformation. The ability to abstract in a meaningful way, in turn, is reliant on the development of critical analytical skills. Studio and seminar program, therefore, stress historical and cultural research along with formal analysis to encourage an inclusive understanding of site and context. This investigation may begin to reveal traces of the society represented in a succession of historical forms, and provide a deeper reading of the evidence that remains. From this material the architect or artist may reassemble another object/city—one that shares an affinity at a more profound level with the object of study than the selection of applique or scenographic representation. Through the abstraction of carefully observed elements a synthetic piece may be produced that can simultaneously recall its lineage and comment on the present.

Opposite page
Nightables, 1987
Resting Towers,
1986–1988
Left
Utopian Prospect,
1988
Following pages
Two Women,
1986–1990
Winesburg, 1989,
a collaboration with
Benjamin Gianni

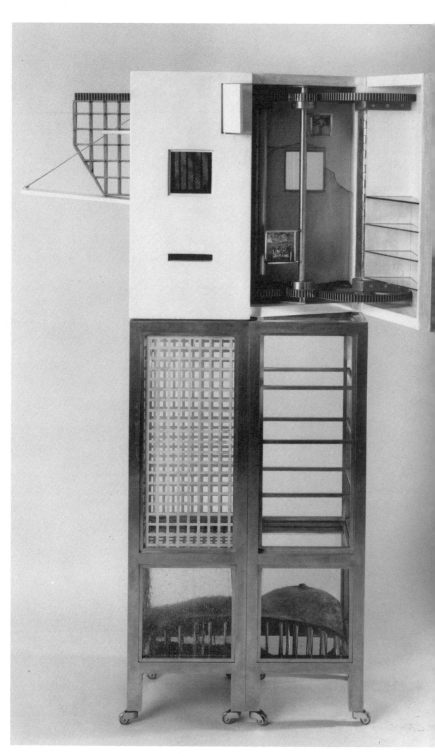

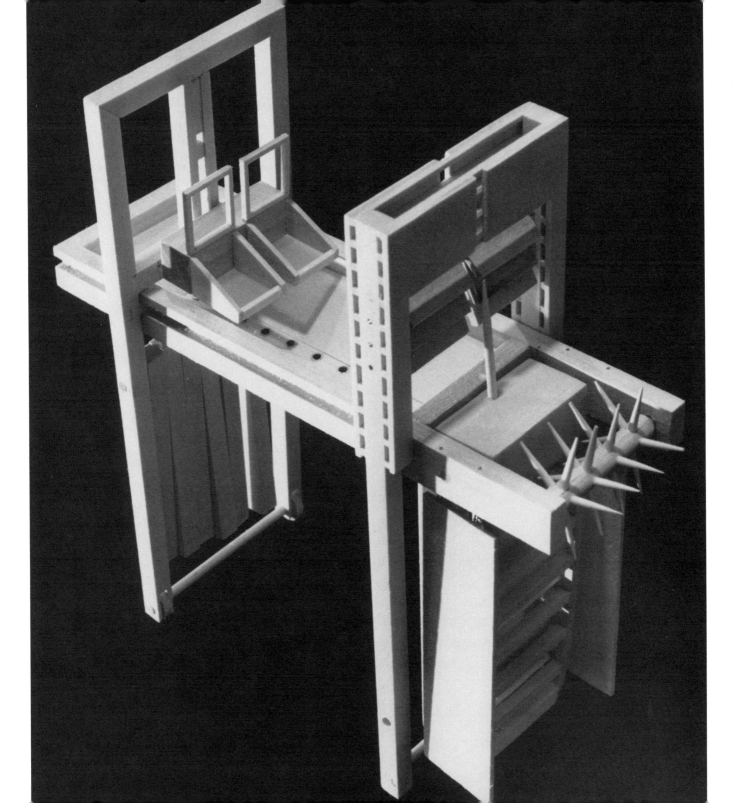

JOEL SANDERS & SCOTT SHERK

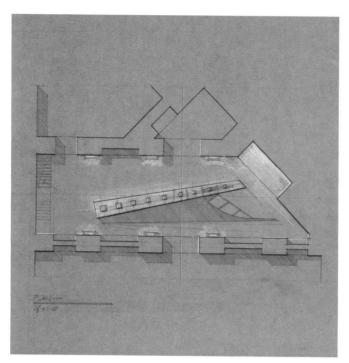

"Architecture is the masterly, correct, and magnificent play of masses brought together in light."—Le Corbusier

Traditionally, both architecture and sculpture alter mass in order to modulate light. In our collaborations, we reverse this process; we alter light in order to modulate and transform mass. We do this by creating shapes and volumes defined by specifically controlled light and shadows cast from carefully placed electric light sources. In our work, we try to draw from some of the common concerns of architecture and sculpture to articulate and transform site specific architectural spaces.

We are teachers as well as practitioners of our respective disciplines. As a result, we are inevitably concerned with the often problematic relationship between theory—what we teach—and practice—what we produce.

The theoretical issues that inform our work focus on art and architecture as products and yet, shapers of culture. We look at how form transmits cultural values and ideologies. Sometimes these values are explicit; more often they are implicit or repressed. Our work tries to expose some of these covert assumptions that are perpetuated through the conventions of architectural and sculptural form.

Our site-specific installations help us look beyond the boundaries of our respective fields. Our work has allowed each of us to see architecture and sculpture from fresh perspectives and different points of view.

Brooklyn Bridge Anchorage

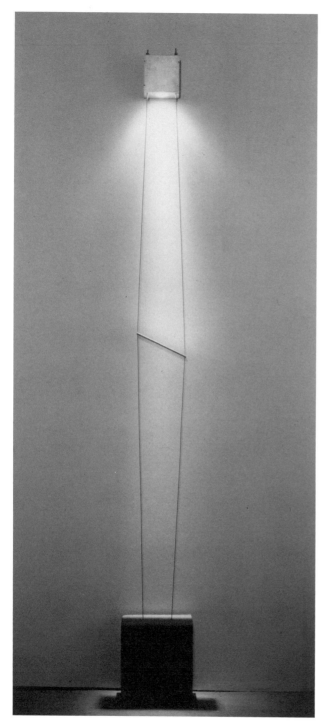

Scott Sherk, **Woman**   **This is not an essence**

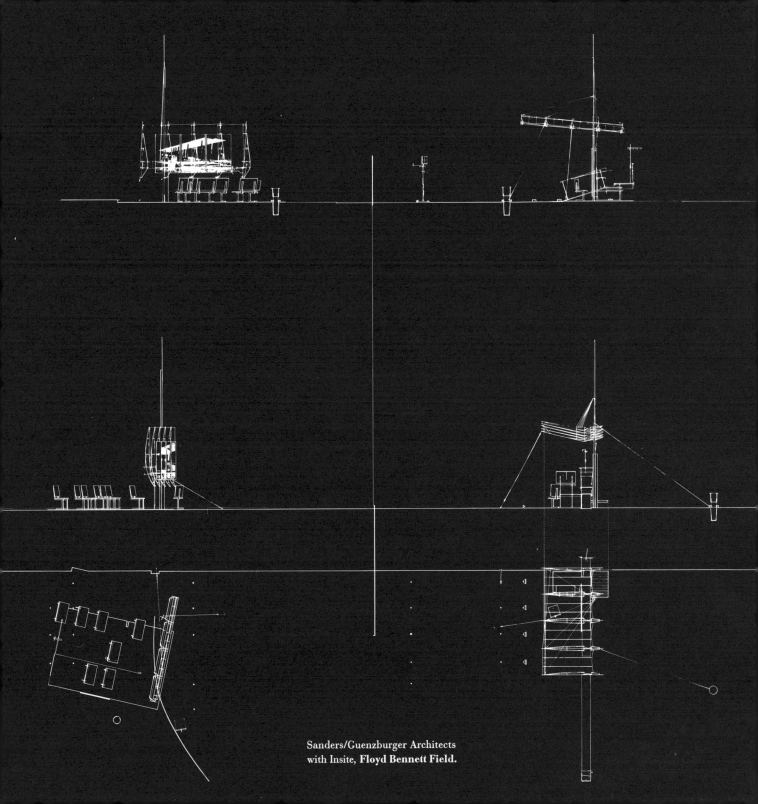

Sanders/Guenzburger Architects
with Insite, **Floyd Bennett Field.**

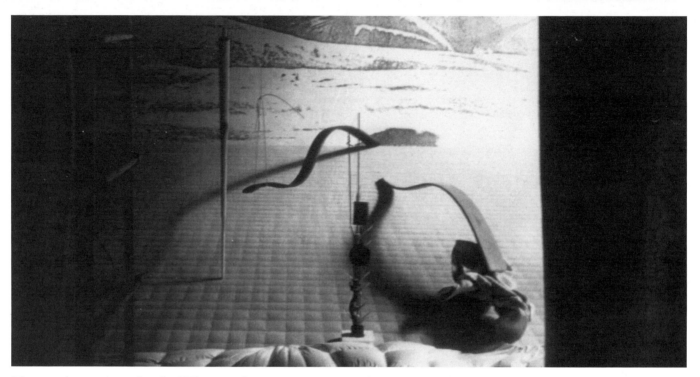

The primary sources for the "Theatre of Amnesia" were Frances Yates' *The Art of Memory* and Spencer's *Memory Palace of Mateo Ricci*. Both of these books deal with the classical memory arts and the architectural structures upon which these arts depended. The necessary fixity of that architecture and the transient nature of the memory images which inhabited it provided the starting point for work on the architecture necessary for an "art of amnesia" (in a manner of speaking).

The sources for the large drawing "A Wounded God Is More Dangerous" are numerous. At the time I was drawing it I was reading several books—books by William Gibson, J.G. Ballard, and William Burroughs. The images that served as the primary "canvas" out of which the drawing emerged were largely fragments of photographs taken from history books.

As far as teaching architecture to my own students is concerned, there is no doubt that eventually, they will each have to locate their own points of departure and sources of illumination, quite apart from my own interests and obsessions. I sincerely hope that whatever impact the sources I have chosen in my own work may have on my students will be strictly temporary. What seems most important to me is the development of a lasting capacity to search out one's own sources of inspiration and, above all, to learn not to be deceived by appearances.

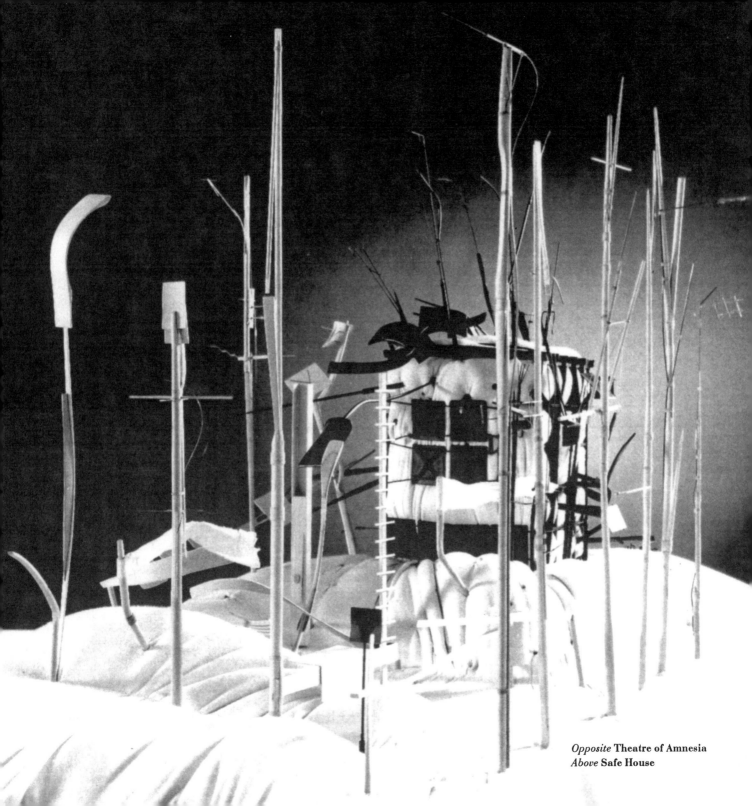

Opposite **Theatre of Amnesia**
Above **Safe House**

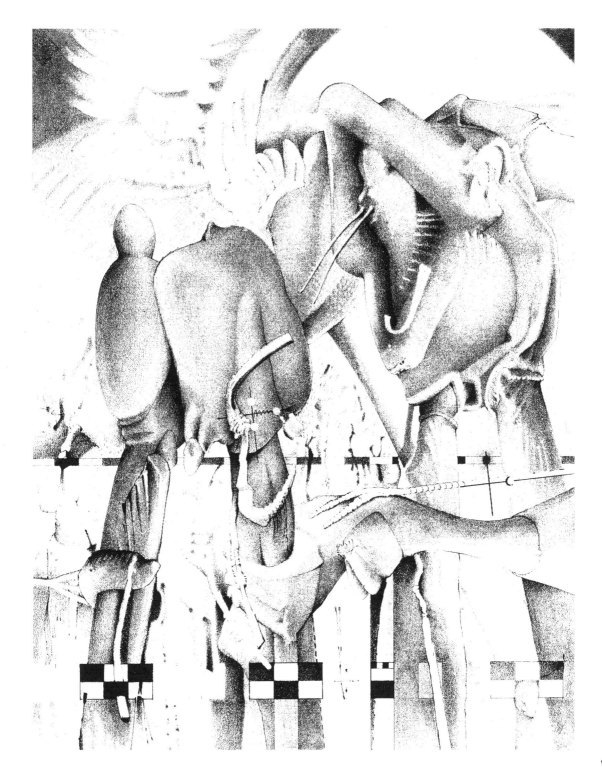

WEST

ROBERT COLE

I hear and I forget
I see and I remember
I do and I understand

This ancient Chinese proverb underscores the necessity of *doing*, which is a fundamental tenet of my professional and pedagogical endeavors. In both, the emphasis is placed on learning. The *doing* of learning begins by asking the appropriate question(s), even before answers are pursued. Such a process inevitably imprints itself on the product. Practicing and teaching architecture represent two facets of the same strategy: the search for the meaning and the making of architecture or, perhaps more cryptically, the pursuit of knowing why we do what we do.

Doing, in the context of my practice, comprises theoretical projects, competitions, and small commissions that provide avenues to explore ideas. The three projects presented—a set design, a jewelry shop, and "The Walking Man," (a lamp-cum-easel-cum-clothes valet)—have all been realized. Radically different in scale and intent, each embraces ideas suggested by an interpretation of the context. Equally, the delight of craftsmanship, in terms of materials and assembly, as well as visual presentation, is inextricably related to the design process. The idea that intention informs realization is critical to the questions posed in the office and in the studio.

Doing, in the context of the design studio, consists of getting a student to think for himself. Projects are set in the general terms of issues, rather than on detailed spatial requirements. Great emphasis is placed on the process of developing a personal 'critical framework' that is based on individual experiences, perceptions, and ultimately, . . . knowledge. This, in turn, grows through participation in the design process. Each student has his own particular gift, or 'answers' to offer. In the briefs submitted, there is a constant exhortation to "think for oneself," to "try it," to do authentic work, rather than "what I, as the critic, want you to do." In the end, it is this type of exploration that proves the best of what we, as architects, have to offer.

In both arenas, the office and the studio, it is the desire to do work of potential consequence that motivates me. Each role—architect or teacher—has its own merits and yet, is intrinsically interdependent with the other. The goal of my teaching is to help students understand *why* they do *what* they do; the goal of my practice is to test and substantiate for myself what I believe in. The critical discourse sharpens my own faculties by providing the place and opportunity to ask questions.

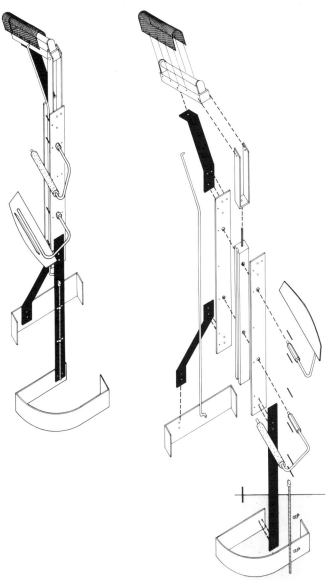

Walking Man

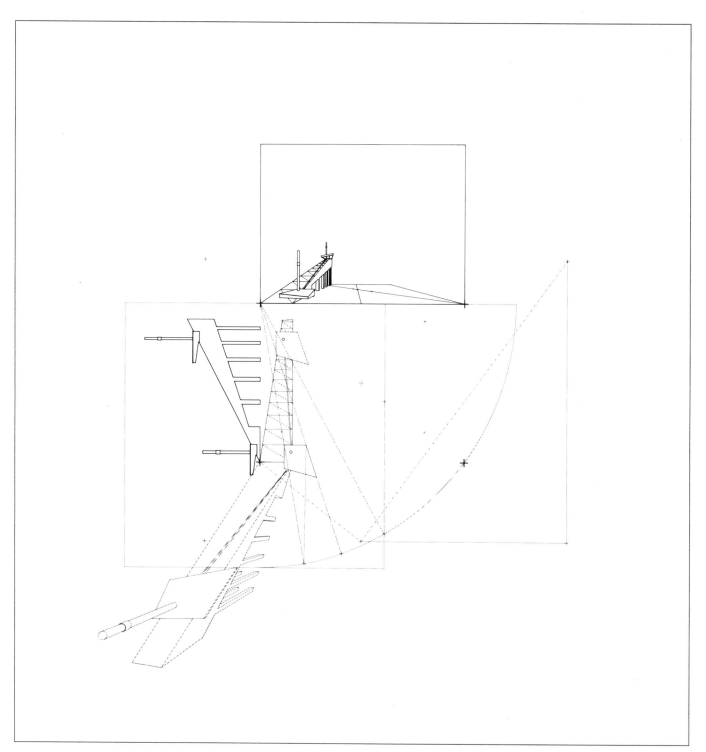

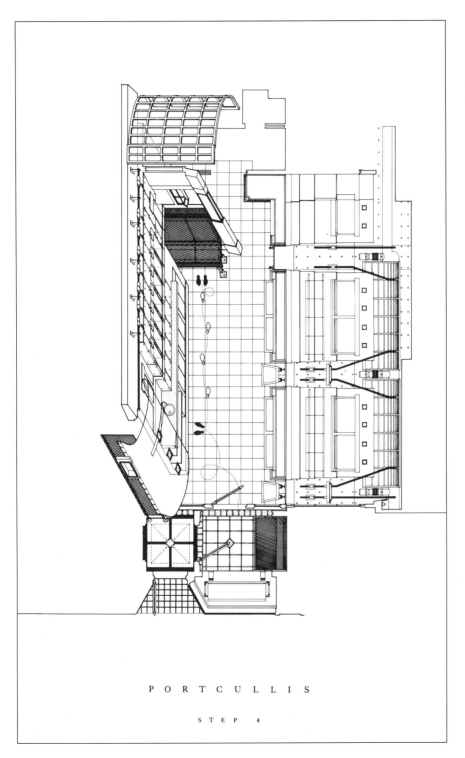

PORTCULLIS

STEP 4

BENJAMIN GIANNI

The work represents an attempt to come to terms with the rural, commercial, and urban landscape of the American Midwest. The issue is a personal as well as a pedagogical one—an attempt to valorize (for myself and for my students) the architecture "at hand" by investigating the "at hand" in the context of broader cultural and philosophical issues. Taking the simplest form of building—the utilitarian building on the arm— as emblematic of structural, material, and iconographic sensibilities of this country, and taking the farm complex as the most primary example of the grouping of buildings to define space, I have been moving toward the American urban environment to investigate the structural and spatial affinities it shares with the farm grouping. One goal is to define a language and logic particular to this architecture and this landscape by which the American urban environment might be elaborated and improved. An attempt is being made to be critical of the built environment of this country on its own terms.

American Fictions, 1989, a collaboration with Mark Robbins.

GIANNI

CAMERON MCNALL

I teach using the Conductor and Orchestra analogy. The challenge is to avoid becoming too familiar with the music. When I lived in New York, I was interested in the relationship between the second and third dimensions and the influence of medium and process on form, shadow, and simulation. Now that I live in Los Angeles, I just go with the flow.

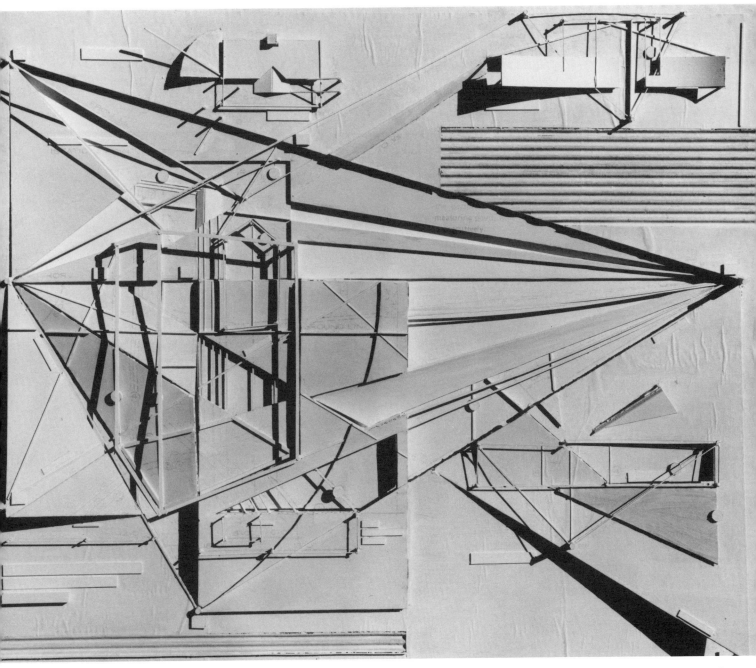

Opposite page **Artpark proposal**
Above **Working drawings**

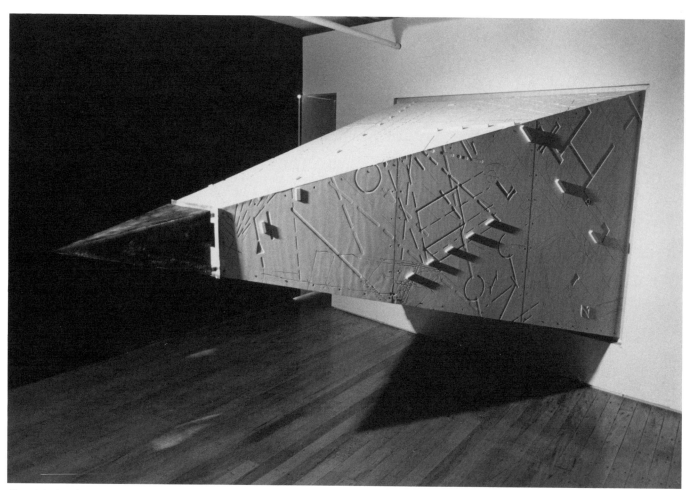

Above **Working Drawings**, installation
Opposite page **Black and White**, installation

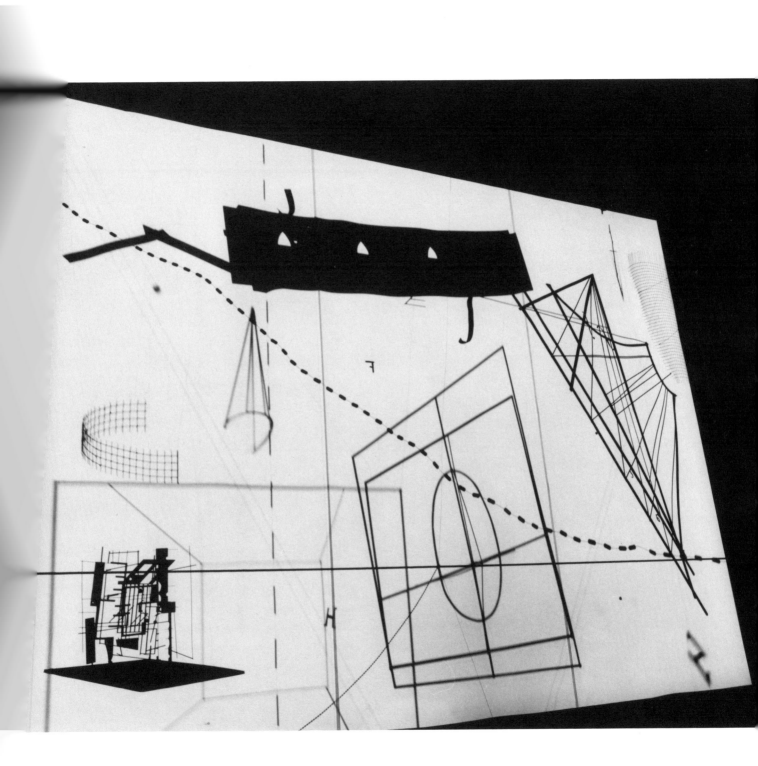

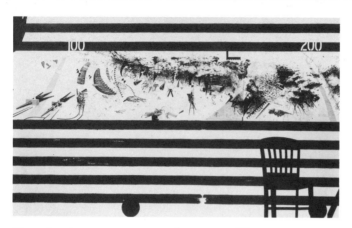

Drawing is an autonomous language. Yet, inspite of the considerable amount of time that the student of architecture spends with pencil in hand, rarely does he observe drawing independent of its employment in the design process. And when this does take place, it is often after the development of the work has run its course and the concern is the "presentation:" drawing as artifact.

If, however, the process of making drawings can be temporarily dislodged from the typical studio situation and looked at "abstractly," there is the possibility that the student will develop a more refined visual literacy. Awareness of the contributory or subversive role that the drawn line plays in graphically thinking about architecture should be second nature. A student so prepared, will get considerably more information *back* from the drawings he produces and in the process becomes a potent critic.

My own work of late has turned toward the exploration of effective drawings of the city. It is my hypothesis that the physical city should be shadowed by a parallel city that exists only on paper, a manual of speculations and revisions that could actually alter one's perception of the built environment. To offer an obvious example of this idea, it is impossible to "see" Rome as it was previous to Piranesi. In fact, so powerful was Piranesi's fiction, that the various fragments which today litter the ruins of the forum have been carefully "placed" to conform to an image conceived through drawing.

It is my intent to force the issues of drawing and the contemporary city. My focus is the edge condition of the city that historically has been delineated by walls and gates. Drawings that speak to this issue and which would be most likely appropriate for this exhibition are still on my desk at the time of this writing. The drawings submitted suggest the foundation upon which the new study will be built.

Below **A Meditation on the Boston Gettysburg Cyclorama**, installation
Opposite page **Drydock #3, An Idle Vessel**

ICA
A ADMINISTRATION
B CONFERENCE
C LIBRARY/CURATORIAL
D PREP SHOP
E LIFT
F SCULPTURE PARK
G SCREEN/STAGE
H GALLERIES

MARINE INDUSTRIAL PARK

SITE

DRYDOCK NO. 3   AN IDLE VESSEL
PROJECT OBJECTIVES   PRESERVATION OF A MONUMENTAL SPACE
SUPPORT MARINE INDUSTRIAL PARK MASTERPLAN
RELOCATION OF THE INSTITUTE OF CONTEMPORARY ART
CREATION OF AN INTERNATIONAL URBAN ART PARK AND PERFORMANCE CENTER

REITER

Tendency to composition in terms of the formal characters makes much contemporary art, in poetry, painting; music, even sculpture and architecture. At their worst, these products are "scientific" rather than artistic; technical exercises, sterile and of a new kind of pedantry. At their best, they assist in ushering in new modes of art and by education of objects; they enlarge and enrich the world of human vision . . . . The creators of such works of art are entitled when successful, to the gratitude that we give to inventors of microscopes and microphones; in the end, they open new object to be observed and enjoyed.

—John Dewey, *Experience, Nature and Art*, 1929

Architecture is a medium of action and implied action in which the designer is only one maker among many in a process. In practice and in training, ideas usually generate a declension of drawings, models and other artifacts including buildings which extend serially towards spatial experience or towards new theoretical territory. In attempting to approximate spatial relationships for others, these works, even in their most expressive forms, often communicate modesty and precision, turning the subject from side to side to depict it from several vantage points, sometimes even maintaining a consistent scale and adhering to conventions of the plan and section diagram. Similarly a continuum of drawings, trace overlays, and tactile manipulations of models are the customary methods of communication between the teacher and student. There is often a freezing/boiling point in the series when models and drawings begin to hoist the idea into another experien-tial or imaginary reality. Two dimensional work can inspire and critique three dimensions work and vice versa. The resonance of these artifacts on other scales of endeavor and in other spatial realities, is in large part responsible for their power and depth, and for their approach to what Dewey called "experience in the form of art."

Architects often do not know their own strength, the power of this medium of action. They have been accused of pandering to the other disciplines, of recasting their own operations within the vocabulary and intentions of, for instance, language or the sciences. Traditionally, the architect may also pursue a parallel strain of finished work in the visual arts as status-giving accoutrement, perhaps implying that the mundane reality of architecture might be transcended by a finer form of artistic expression. Meanwhile, visual artists like Vito Acconci or James Turrell have recognized the powers of architecture, of public contact, a palette of form, light and space, and potentially, a sensual reality beyond the aesthetic deep freeze of the gallery.

Bearings was designed to be an exhibition which considered artifacts of an architectural or interdisciplinary process as it relates to pedagogy in design schools across the nation. Perhaps architecture should command its own form of exhibition with its own requirements and concerns peculiar to an experiential as well as a visual art form. The *Bearings* show has only reached a fraction of its potential in this regard given that all of the submissions were placed in a gallery and were, for the most part, treated like objects from one branch of the visual arts. Still, one aim of the selection and curatorial process was to emphasize the variety of submissions, especially since recent architectural exhibitions have tended towards art historical categorization of design trends, and the works, taken together, had a remarkable effect on each other. *Bearings* was not an exhibition of architecture on ice, but rather was admirably something more like a science fair or an exhibit of hybrid strains of similar species.

In many ways the show represented a generation of young teachers engaged in altering the received architectural pedantry of recent generations, perhaps recognizing that the aesthetic framing of architecture as a drawn composition of sign and symbol, as engraved plate or gallery object, runs counter to the strength of the process and offers little to empower the student. Some *Bearings* submissions were rarified statements about one aspect of the architectural process, holding it up for special consideration as a trace element lacking within the diet of architectural thought or de-emphasized in recent architectural discourse. In other cases the submissions were part of an empathetic process of relieving the architect of self-importance by intersecting with other disciplines to challenge or contaminate the design process with outside intelligence, broaden the palette, and demonstrate that architecture is, more than anything, a potential to be filled and refilled with different ingredients.

In general, though there was great topical variety in the submissions, many began by suspending preconceived notions of spatial experience and perception, finding fluid unknown territory in which to conduct new explorations of these ideas. Almost all of the exhibitors included three dimensional objects, some of which were inhabitable or scaled to the viewer. The models experimented with complex geometries, hetero-geneous organizations, and spatial sleight of hand. Other small scale architectural/sculptural models, presented movable parts to be operated by the viewer, or engaged the viewer in looking through an aperture, thus generating form around activity or some basic parameter of perception. Some works reconsidered light as volume and form; others were involved in introducing new hybrid mixtures of materials to explore texture and surface as well as interactions between internal structural forces. Some sited their work off of new perceptions of the elemental forces of water, atmosphere and geography; others positioned architecture in terms of political action. In a very few cases, the submissions might be considered actual by-products of a design process with students.

The teacher who advances into uncharted territory with successive stages of objectification emphasizes the importance of *making* at a scale of endeavor which intersects with that of the student. And there is the potential for a real apprenticeship in an intuitive or integrative method—apprenticeship in discovering a personal design process. Models and other small objects used in pedagogical conversation, through the professor's work, also become objects that can be seen as one stage in the process of building. There is substantial strength in the theoretical idea glimpsed through a tangible object in light and air. Similarly, amongst architecture teachers, exhibitions like *Bearings* are perhaps a concise and powerful form of exchange which the academic paper or studio jury cannot approach.

Bearings will continue in the coming years. It is important that the show not encourage merely another form of pedantry with a different palette and a slightly different set of concerns. In the future, entrants might require an installation of spatial experience that is more demonstrative than illustrative, more in keeping with the powers of the discipline. Architecture studio as an ongoing guerrilla exhibition, is itself a very charged precedent for a new way of exhibiting the work. Within the current parameters of the show, the spontaneous happening might be somewhat artificial, but it is possible to show that the artifacts do not stand alone, but that they are rather part of a process that extends beyond the gallery. *Bearings* may also begin to survey a broader range of regional concern, modes of representation and most importantly, different *activities* which require training in the discipline of architecture.